Christopher Wren

Very Interesting People

*Bite-sized biographies of Britain's most
fascinating historical figures*

CURRENTLY AVAILABLE

1. **William Shakespeare** *Peter Holland*
2. **George Eliot** *Rosemary Ashton*
3. **Charles Dickens** *Michael Slater*
4. **Charles Darwin** *Adrian Desmond, James Moore,
    and Janet Browne*
5. **Isaac Newton** *Richard S. Westfall*
6. **Elizabeth I** *Patrick Collinson*
7. **George III** *John Cannon*
8. **Benjamin Disraeli** *Jonathan Parry*
9. **Christopher Wren** *Kerry Downes*
10. **John Ruskin** *Robert Hewison*

FORTHCOMING

11. **James Joyce** *Bruce Stewart*
12. **John Milton** *Gordon Campbell*
13. **Jane Austen** *Marilyn Butler*
14. **Henry VIII** *E. W. Ives*
15. **Queen Victoria** *H. C. G. Matthew and
    K. D. Reynolds*
16. **Winston Churchill** *Paul Addison*
17. **Oliver Cromwell** *John Morrill*
18. **Thomas Paine** *Mark Philp*
19. **J. M. W. Turner** *Luke Herrmann*
20. **William and Mary** *Tony Claydon and W. A. Speck*

Christopher Wren

Very Interesting People

Kerry Downes

OXFORD
UNIVERSITY PRESS

OXFORD
UNIVERSITY PRESS

Great Clarendon Street, Oxford ox2 6DP

Oxford University Press is a department of the University of Oxford.
It furthers the University's objective of excellence in research, scholarship,
and education by publishing worldwide in

Oxford New York

Auckland Cape Town Dar es Salaam Hong Kong Karachi
Kuala Lumpur Madrid Melbourne Mexico City Nairobi
New Delhi Shanghai Taipei Toronto

With offices in

Argentina Austria Brazil Chile Czech Republic France Greece
Guatemala Hungary Italy Japan Poland Portugal Singapore
South Korea Switzerland Thailand Turkey Ukraine Vietnam

Oxford is a registered trade mark of Oxford University Press
in the UK and in certain other countries

Published in the United States
by Oxford University Press Inc., New York

First published in the *Oxford Dictionary of National Biography* 2004
This paperback edition first published 2007

British Library Cataloguing in Publication Data

Data available

Library of Congress Cataloging in Publication Data

Data available

Typeset by SPI Publisher Services, Pondicherry, India
Printed in Great Britain
on acid-free paper by
Ashford Colour Press Ltd., Gosport, Hants.

ISBN 978–0–19–921524–9 (Pbk.)

10 9 8 7 6 5 4 3 2 1

Contents

Preface vii

1 A man of science and invention 1

2 Making of an architect 19

3 The City churches and St Paul's 33

4 A public architect 51

5 Mechanical hand and
    philosophical mind 69

Sources 85

Index 87

Preface

There is always something more to be said. In five years Wren's masterpiece, St Paul's Cathedral, has changed dramatically. Exterior recleaning, still in progress, has restored the way in which the mouldings and relief details 'read', how each piece fits into a visual structure partly representing, partly expressing, the material structure of mass and support. It restores clarity and balance, like removing scratch from old records, or brown varnish from a painting. The interior cleaning, finished first, is even more dramatic, taking away the deepest traces of the soot that was already eating into the stonework before the cathedral was finished, and the last remnants of the three coats of oil paint Wren had ordered at the eleventh hour in an attempt to hide the dirt and the many surface patches that it affected unevenly. Now the patches are hardly noticeable, and the whole interior has the luminosity—from direct daylight combined with reflected light from one bright stone to another—that Wren envisaged but, after thirty-five years in building, never saw. The soul has come back to St Paul's.

The most interesting challenge for me when writing this short life, originally for the *Oxford Dictionary of National Biography*, was Wren the scientist. I hope I have met it adequately. Recent work on the role of intuition in the work of various architects has helped me understand that Wren's brilliance, on which contemporaries remarked, lay in the intuitive capacity he was loath to acknowledge. This does not seem to have *scared* him, but he could not explain it. Neuropsychology still cannot explain how the brain processes numerical quantities—an operation of which numbers on paper or a screen are merely symbols, as words and syntax are symbolic of verbal thought. Great leaps in mathematics come unexpectedly, in a flash (as

Poincaré vividly related) and I am now convinced that what Wren did after the Warrant design for St Paul's was similar. The added height and light inside, the two-storey exterior elevation, and changes in the scale of the whole: the unit was no longer generated from a fraction of the building or the column, like the unclimbable steps of the Parthenon, but by reference to the human figure.

Finally, Wren's use of the Roman calendar system proves that his 'old-style' Easter holiday for 1649 was in England, not abroad: he never did see St Peter's in Rome.

Kerry Downes

August 2006

About the author

Kerry Downes is Professor Emeritus of the History of Art, University of Reading; the author of many books on Wren and his contemporaries, he is currently writing a study on Borromini.

A man of science and invention

1

Sir Christopher Wren (1632–1723), architect, mathematician, and astronomer, was born at East Knoyle, Wiltshire, on 20 October 1632, the only surviving son of Christopher Wren DD (1589–1658), at that time rector of East Knoyle and later dean of Windsor, and his wife, Mary, the daughter of Richard Cox of Fonthill, Wiltshire. His paternal grandfather, Francis Wren (1553–1624), was a London mercer, but the family came from Durham and, they believed, originally from Denmark. A previous child, born on 22 November 1631 and baptized Christopher, had died the same day; the antiquary John Aubrey's confusion of the two persisted occasionally into late twentieth-century literature. The surviving

copy of the parish register is misleading, but
Dr Wren's copy of Christoph Helwig's *Theatrum
historicum* (1618; National Library of Wales,
Aberystwyth) contains his accurate family record
even to the hour of birth.

Early life and education

As a child Wren 'seem'd consumptive' (Wren,
346)—the kind of sickly child who survives into
robust old age. He was first taught at home by
a private tutor, the Revd William Shepheard,
and by his father, a man of scholarly aspirations
and wide interests including natural philosophy,
mathematics, and architecture. After Dr Wren's
appointment as dean of Windsor in March 1635
his family spent part of each year there, but about
1639 he engaged a plasterer to embellish the
chancel walls of East Knoyle church with plaster
reliefs and pietistic inscriptions. This work survives, but of the 'very strong roof' he made at
Knoyle neither the location nor the survival is
known.

The Laudian high Anglicanism which brought Dr Wren preferment in 1635 was to become an embarrassment. He was more fortunate than his elder brother Matthew Wren (1585–1667), bishop of Ely, who was imprisoned for twenty years. However, in the autumn of 1642 parliamentary soldiers searched the Windsor deanery, seizing the treasury of the Order of the Garter of which the dean was registrar, and many personal effects. He took refuge at Knoyle and, while it supported the king, at Bristol.

Little is known about Wren's schooling. According to John Aubrey, Sir Christopher determined to give his own son—also Christopher—the public education he himself had not received. The story that he was at Westminster School from 1641 to 1646 is unsubstantiated; *Parentalia* (1750), compiled by the younger Christopher, states that his father was there 'for some short time' before going to Oxford (in 1650). According to *Parentalia* Wren was 'initiated' in the principles of mathematics by Dr William Holder, who became rector of Bletchingdon, Oxfordshire, in 1642 and married Wren's elder sister Susan the following year. Although, according to Aubrey, in adulthood he was no great reader, Wren received a thorough grounding in Latin; he also learned to draw. Some youthful exercises are preserved or recorded (though few are datable); his earliest talents were for Latin composition and for devising graphic and other visual aids. In his tenth year he wrote a new year greeting for his father in Latin prose and verse, directed *E musaeo meo*, while from his early teens two projects survive for hand-signing alphabets for deaf people. One is titled (in Greek) *Cheirologia*, suggesting a prompt response to the proposition in William Bulwer's *Chirologia* (1644), only taken up in print in 1661 by George Dalgarno. Instructing deaf people was a preoccupation of Holder, and the mutual interest suggests that he may have contributed to Wren's education even before his marriage, as well as after 1646 when the Wren family, finally evicted from Knoyle, lodged with the Holders at Bletchingdon; Dean Wren remained there until his death on 29 May 1658.

Work of this period included a design for a 'pneumatic engine' or air pump (later perfected by Robert Boyle), a pasteboard star calendar, a *sciotericon* to plot equal hours from a sundial, a device for writing in the dark, a recording weather clock, and a pasteboard calculator for the orbit of the moon. Bletchingdon is not far from Oxford, and it was probably through Holder that Wren met there the physician and natural philosopher, Sir Charles Scarburgh. He assisted Scarburgh in his anatomical studies, and in a letter of 1647 Wren acknowledged his gratitude to the physician not only for his teaching but also, in a recent unspecified illness, for saving his life. Before 1648 he was making paste-board models to illustrate Scarburgh's lectures on muscular action, and translating into Latin, at Scarburgh's suggestion, William Oughtred's tract on dialling or gnomonics, for a new Latin edition (1652) of Oughtred's *Clavis mathematicae*. Already a common thread appears in Wren's interests: mechanics, anatomy, and applied mathematics, and the preference for practical results and visual demonstrations that would lead him to architecture.

Wren entered Wadham College, Oxford, on 25 June 1650. His choice was probably influenced, through Holder and Scarburgh, by Wadham's strength in mathematics and natural science under the wardenship of John Wilkins, appointed the previous year after a term as chaplain to Charles Louis, elector palatine. (As a child, Wren had met the elector when he was a visitor to the Windsor deanery, but he did not meet Wilkins who was not then in the elector's service.) At Wadham, Wren's formal education was conventional; his informal studies were at least as important. The Oxford curriculum was still based on the study of Aristotle and the discipline of the Latin language, and it is anachronistic to imagine that he received scientific training in the modern sense. But as a gentleman commoner he could dine at the fellows' table, and Wilkins was host to the circle of distinguished scholars, of varied though moderate political persuasion who, soon after the Restoration, formed jointly with a similar group in London the nucleus of the Royal Society. Original and sometimes brilliant practical workers, experimental philosophers in the mould publicized earlier in the century by Francis Bacon and later by Thomas Sprat, Wilkins's circle included at various times the mathematicians Seth Ward, John Wallis, and Robert Wood, the experimenters Boyle and Robert Hooke, the physicians Jonathan Goddard and Thomas Willis, and the astronomer Lawrence Rooke.

Scientific work in Oxford and London

Wren graduated BA on 18 March 1651 and MA on 14 December 1653. As an undergraduate he designed a box-beehive and a practical hygrometer, and contributed twenty lines of florid and allusive verse to a collection celebrating William Petty's resuscitation of a hanged Oxford woman (R. Watkins, ed., *Newes from the Dead*, Oxford, 1651). Election to a fellowship at All Souls College on 3 November 1653 ensured the continuation of his research, although he was often in London. John Evelyn visited him in Oxford in July 1654 noting—as did others—his close collaboration with John Wilkins, who shared and fostered his interest in mechanical devices and demonstrations. With Wilkins's encouragement Wren developed an instrument for writing two copies of a document at once, and drew from the image in a microscope; he also caught Wilkins's enthusiasm for telescopes, and after 1654 interest in computational astronomy ceded to optical. In 1655 they built an 80 foot instrument for observing the whole face of the moon.

Early in his fellowship Wren developed a perspectograph or scenographic apparatus, in which, by a movable sight linked to a pen, a view could be traced on paper; later, in 1663, he showed this device to the Royal Society, and prototypes were built. By 1657 he had persuaded Boyle to test Descartes's hypothesis that atmospheric pressure varied, like the tides, with lunar influence—this was before Newton's law of gravitation. Boyle's experiments disproved the hypothesis and led to the advance of the barometer from a philosophical curiosity to a useful instrument. Wren's anatomical studies included dissections of fish and other creatures, and experiments about 1656 with intravenous injection into animals. Incorporating earlier observations and using newly improved optics, he studied the appearance and phases of Saturn sufficiently to draft a monograph on the subject, but promptly abandoned it when he received advance news of Christiaan Huygens's hypothesis (*Systema Saturnium*, 1659).

Wren continued to divide his time between Oxford and London, as he would do well into the 1660s. On 7 August 1657 he was appointed to the chair of astronomy at Gresham College in the City of London, apparently on the recommendation of Wilkins to Oliver Cromwell, whose widowed sister Wilkins had recently married. Cromwell intervened personally in the appointment, Lawrence Rooke, the current holder, being assigned the chair of geometry to accommodate him. Gresham was noted for mathematical study, especially applied mathematics (including navigation, which Wren was required to teach). He subsequently lectured on light, Saturn, and

Johannes Kepler, and on dioptrics, the nascent science of lenses named by Kepler and amplified by Descartes.

The Gresham lecture

Wren's inaugural lecture of August 1657 survives in disparate Latin and English versions (printed in Ward and *Parentalia* respectively); it is the only account of his view of the sciences. Both versions are carefully composed. His tributes to the founder, Sir Thomas Gresham, to previous professors, to the City, and to the muse of astronomy are gracious, well turned, and apt; Wren enumerated, with examples familiar to an educated audience, the practical applications and benefits of his discipline, especially to trade and industry. The most important passages, however, give a more personal and individual view of the 'new philosophy', its invention, its foundations, and its heroic figures. This, Wren claimed, had liberated all the sciences from the intellectual constraints of ancient Greek and Roman thought, but astronomy was particularly firmly supported: on the one hand by the absolute authority of mathematical truth, on the other hand by the new disciplines of magnetics, initiated by William Gilbert, and dioptrics. Mathematical demonstrations:

> being built upon the impregnable Foundations of Geometry and Arithmetick, are the only Truths, that can sink into the Mind of Man, void of all Uncertainty; and all other Discourses participate more or less of truth, according as their Subjects are more or less capable of Mathematical Demonstration. (Wren, 200–01)

Indeed for Wren logic was but a branch of mathematics, and to the latter he awarded the Aristotelian title of *organon organōn*, or instrument of instruments. Wren understood the earlier reference to Aristotle in the title of Francis Bacon's *Novum organum* (1620) and Bacon's vision of a new science founded on inductive reasoning from observation and experiment. However, although by the mid-seventeenth century it was commonplace both to acknowledge Bacon and to disown Aristotle, Wren did neither, not even mentioning

Bacon. The 'new science' was not attributable solely to Bacon, its herald rather than its inventor. Mathematics is deductive, one reason why Bacon, the advocate of induction, neglected it; moreover, mathematics in general and geometry in particular involve intuitive as well as logical thought, and here Wren's position is explicitly distinct from Bacon's. He praises Copernicus, Kepler, Galileo, and Descartes, but calls Gilbert the 'Father of the new Philosophy' in preference to Descartes, 'but a Builder upon his [Gilbert's] Experiments' (Wren, 204). He ranks the physiologist William Harvey equally with Gilbert, noting that both are English and adding a reference to 'the useful Invention of Logarithms...wholy a British Art' (ibid., 206). He also repudiates the occult science of his time, in which several of his colleagues showed more than a passing interest. He condemns 'the ungrounded Fancies of...astrological Medicasters' (*pseudomedici* and 'quack astrologers'; ibid., 202). Little weight, therefore, can be placed on his occasional interest in strange phenomena (he once cured a sickness by eating dates after dreaming of them) or from his attendance at the Oxford

chemistry classes of the hermetist Peter Staehl;
most of his circle did likewise.

Wren's growing reputation

Wren was in contact with Parisian scholars
by 1658, when Blaise Pascal challenged the
mathematicians of Europe with two problems
concerning differential curves. The first was the
calculation of line, area, and other quantities of
a cycloid—the arc traced by a point on the cir-
cumference of a travelling wheel. The second
was to derive, from given dimensions, the length
of a chord across an ellipse. Wren partly solved
both problems, which were germane to the understanding of planetary orbits. However, in the first
he substituted simpler values than those specified,
and in both he offered not the numerical solutions required but geometrical constructions from
which they could be derived. In counter-challenge
he re-presented a problem of Kepler's concerning
ellipses. Pascal commended his work but withheld
the prizes, as Wren had not satisfied the conditions. He was still working in London and Oxford;

in 1659 he was a bursar of All Souls, and designed and set up the sundial, carved by William Byrd, on the south wall of the chapel—reset in 1877 on the college's Codrington Library (H. Colvin and J. S. G. Simmons, *All Souls*, 1989, 70–71).

A list in *Parentalia* of Wren's inventions before 1660 includes devices for surveying, musical and acoustical instruments, developments in fishing, underwater construction and submarine navigation, and experiments in printmaking; he experimented with, but did not invent, the mezzotint technique, which Prince Rupert demonstrated to the Royal Society in 1661. Wren found it prudent to stay in Oxford when, in the anarchy after the resignation of Richard Cromwell, Commonwealth troops occupied Gresham College (in October 1659, not a year earlier as often assumed). Life at Gresham returned to normal with the Restoration, but within a year Wren had resigned his chair. On 5 February 1661 he was elected to the Savilian chair of astronomy at Oxford in succession to Seth Ward, and on 12 September he received a doctorate in civil law. The Restoration brought other changes. Wren's uncle Matthew was released from the Tower and his cousin the younger Matthew received a court appointment. The Wadham and Gresham circles became the nucleus of the Royal Society, inaugurated at a meeting after Christopher's Gresham lecture on 28 November 1660; thereafter he helped to draw up the society's royal charter. Charles II's initial enthusiasm for the new science stemmed not only from natural curiosity—his salad days had perforce been curtailed by affairs of state—but also from the political function he envisaged for the society in mending ideological bridges, uniting minds of diverse faction in the common cause of a single nation.

Wren came particularly to the king's notice through the Royal Society and his use of optics. In May 1661 the society forwarded a royal command to accomplish two projects he had begun, based on optics. From telescopic observations Wren was modelling a relief globe of the moon, as big as a human head; he was also the first Englishman to make microscopical drawings of minute creatures.

Neither project survives, though both were completed; the drawings of insects hanging at Whitehall Palace in 1688 probably perished in the fire of 1698. In the autumn of 1661 Wren assigned his microscopy to Robert Hooke, who in *Micrographia* (1665) acknowledged him as its originator. At the same time Wren was approached by his cousin Matthew with a royal commission, as 'one of the best Geometricians in Europe', to direct the refortification of Tangier, ceded by Portugal as part of the queen's dowry. Wren excused himself on grounds of health, and a military engineer was subsequently engaged.

However, before the end of 1661 Wren was unofficially advising on the repair of old St Paul's Cathedral after two decades of neglect and distress, and this assignment took temporary precedence over his duties as Savilian professor. But in 1662 he lectured on spheres, on the date of Easter (*De paschate*, not on Pascal as often stated), and on navigation—appropriate topics when mathematics was increasingly seen as the key to all scientific knowledge. Later Oxford lectures are unrecorded, but Royal Society and other sources show the drift of his studies in the next three years: graphite for lubricating timepieces; a mechanical corn drill; a self-regulating weather clock recording temperature and wind direction; an egg incubator; a demonstration model of an eye—based on that of a horse—as proposed by Descartes with a translucent retina. He also worked on a theory of elastic impact from the collision of balls suspended by threads, on respiration and the vital principle of air (a subject not fathomed until the discovery of oxygen over a century later), and on tracking the comets of 1664–5, then believed to travel in a straight line. In collaboration with Thomas Willis he made drawings from dissections, beautiful in themselves and remarkably accurate and informative, including those of the brain engraved for Willis's *Cerebri anatome* (1664). In 1664 he was incorporated MA at Cambridge.

Making of an architect

First steps to architecture

It was not unusual in this period for the well-educated to take up architecture as a gentlemanly activity, widely accepted in theory as a branch of applied mathematics; this is implicit in the writings of Vitruvius and explicit in such sixteenth-century authors as John Dee and Leonard Digges. Wren's father was a keen and erudite observer of buildings. Oxford saw much fine building throughout the first half of the seventeenth century, and Wren's own college, Wadham, was a paragon of Jacobean modernity (1610–13). He arrived at Gresham with a far from casual eye, having in Oxford absorbed intuitively the fundamentals of architectural design.

He was also familiar with Vitruvius's *De archi-tectura*; *Parentalia* mentions among his pre-1660 work 'new designs tending to strength, conveni-ence and beauty in building', confirming knowl-edge of Vitruvius's tripartite formula. It remained only for him to realize that architecture could be the supreme demonstration of the truths he had championed in his Gresham lecture.

The invitation to superindent Tangier's refortifi-cation may have arisen from Charles II's casual opportunism in matching people to tasks; how-ever, Wren was already on the way to architec-tural practice. The reward offered was certainly significant—the reversion of the surveyorship of the royal works on the death of Sir John Denham (1615–1669). Denham's appointment had been opportunistic, service to the king in exile counting for more than familiarity with building. On the other hand, by 1661 Wren's architectural interests were evident to his associates and would not have escaped an observer as shrewd as Charles. In later years Wren complained to his son that Charles had done him a disservice in making him an architect, and that he would have made a better living in medicine. Nevertheless he must have known that the king's judgement and his own compliance had been right. By the early 1660s he had mastered architecture and understood it thoroughly. Several colleagues might have taken it up as a set of rules and formulas for design, but he alone—and to a lesser extent Robert Hooke—possessed, understood, and exploited the combination of reason and intuition, experience and imagination essential to what we call genius.

This is the setting for Wren's only foreign journey, to Paris and the Île-de-France; he left London in late June 1665 and did not return until early March 1666. He incidentally avoided most of the plague, but he had made plans months earlier; his motives reflect his range of interests. His name was known and respected in Paris, and for a distinguished member of the Royal Society, armed with useful introductions, the strengthening of foreign correspondence would have been sufficient reason to travel. Another was more cogent—first-hand study of contemporary European architecture. He was already designing and supervising buildings, and although records of his journey are sparse—primarily one long letter from Wren himself—the two figures he expressly wished to meet, and undoubtedly met, were the French architect François Mansart and the Italian sculptor and architect G. L. Bernini, who arrived in Paris from Rome at the request of Louis XIV on 2 June 1665. On his return Wren wrote of 'daily conference with the best Artists', French and Italian, and first-hand study of modern design and construction cannot have attracted him less than the prospect of meeting scientific colleagues.

Early commissions

By 1663 Wren was confident enough, and well enough known to close associates, to put theory into practice with two commissions. In 1663 his uncle Matthew gave Pembroke College, Cambridge, a new chapel, a modest building whose interior (extended in 1880 by George Gilbert Scott) is conventional, with classically inspired plasterwork and joinery of a high standard. It was consecrated in Wren's absence on 21 September 1665, but he was certainly in overall charge of the work. The exterior required a street front without a portal, access being from the court, and Wren made a novel adaptation of a small Roman temple front from Serlio's *Architettura*.

Wren's understanding of structures and of the classical language of architecture, his empirical and innovative attitude to prototypes, and his regard for the particulars of his brief were all manifested in a more substantial work, the Sheldonian Theatre, Oxford, proposed and ultimately paid for by Archbishop Gilbert Sheldon, formerly warden of All Souls. Contemporaries associated this building with the Royal Society, to whom Wren showed a wooden model (now lost) of his design on 29 April 1663. That design, always said (through a misreading of *Parentalia*, p. 335) to have derived from the theatre of Marcellus in Rome, was apparently intended not only for the academic ceremonies but also for both anatomy demonstrations and the staging of plays. Site work began the following spring, and on 26 July 1664 the foundation stone was laid for a different design. The theatre's U-shaped plan recalls a Roman theatre less than does Robert Streater's illusionist ceiling depicting the canvas *velarium* pulled back to reveal a sky full of allegorical figures. There is no stage, and the big high windows, raked seating, and unobscured vision proper to an anatomy theatre make an ideal setting for the real spectacle of academic ceremonial. These features were the core of Wren's brief, and although contemporaries recognized his use of Renaissance architectural language as more advanced than elsewhere in Oxford, function was his guiding principle in a building for which there was no typical precedent to follow. His restriction of the classical orders outside to the entrance front thus stemmed from scepticism of received ideas rather than from ignorance or inexperience. To span the interior without intermediate pillars he devised a system of modified king-post trusses connected by bolts and scarf joints, widely believed by contemporaries to reflect the latest mechanical theories but actually derived from traditional roof carpentry. The theatre was inaugurated on

9–10 July 1669; John Evelyn, who attended, recorded the ceremonies in his diary. Both the public spaces and the hidden ones under the seating galleries were also used by the university press, and for many years after the construction of Nicholas Hawksmoor's Clarendon building (1712–13) books still bore the imprint 'At the Theatre'.

The Savilian professor's talents were noticed by colleagues. In 1664 he designed a chapel screen for All Souls (rebuilt and transformed by Sir James Thornhill, 1716); this was followed by screens at St John's (c.1670, destroyed 1848) and Merton colleges (1671–3, partly reinstated 1960)—three different and skilful classical insertions into Gothic interiors. Trinity College built to his design a detached range of rooms in the garden (1665–8); the core of this remains, with later additions. A similar range at the Queen's College (1671–4) survives in essence. At Emmanuel College, Cambridge, the new chapel and cloister range was conceived by William Sancroft, briefly master before becoming dean of St Paul's. With Sancroft in London and Wren either there or in Oxford, progress was at first slow. Building began in 1668 according to a wooden model, and although the structure was finished in 1673 (date on façade) the furnishing delayed the consecration until September 1677. The cloister closes the back of the first court, with a gallery above and the west end wall of the chapel (based on the earlier one at Pembroke) forming the centrepiece. Wren again followed the spirit rather than the letter of classical design, producing an original solution where neither the nature of the site nor the repertory of antiquity offered an obvious precedent.

An established architect

Wren might never have been more than the first of a line of Oxford scholars with architectural interests, but for two circumstances: the great fire of London and his appointment as surveyor-general of the king's works. The fire changed the problem of St Paul's from practical repair and ideal fantasy to complete rebuilding over thirty-five years; it also caused the replacement of many of the City's parish churches. Although he had assistants in both, St Paul's is Wren's cathedral and its lesser neighbours will always be known as the Wren churches.

His appointment as surveyor of the king's works on 29 March 1669 gave Wren status, command of the largest building organization in the country, and creative opportunities limited solely—if strictly—by the exchequer. Because of a recent reform his surveyorship was at the monarch's pleasure and not for life, but he was retained for almost four decades. He is often stated to have become Denham's deputy in 1661 (an error at least as old as Horace Walpole's *Anecdotes of Painting in England*, 1762–71), but he did so only during the last weeks of Denham's life. However, Charles II had engaged him privately in 1664 to make a design for rebuilding Whitehall Palace. The king sketched the design for Evelyn, but the only official records are a bill for a wooden model and a corresponding drawing in Wren's hand. This episode left no doubt of Wren's ability, and the 1669 appointment confirmed a process which had begun in 1661. Wren received an official house in Scotland Yard, where he lived and worked until 1718. On 7 December 1669 he married, at the Temple Church, Faith (1636–1675), the daughter of Sir Thomas Coghill; as her family home was Bletchingdon they had probably known each other for some years.

Wren never abandoned his scientific interests, and although he attended fewer Royal Society meetings he often spoke. During the later 1660s and early 1670s he addressed the society on topics including the mechanics of muscular action, the physiology of flies, and an improved friction brake for winding gear. In December 1668 he produced his theory, or 'law of nature', of the collision of bodies, which he had formulated several years earlier. In June 1669 he demonstrated a machine for grinding aspherical lenses; optical theory showed that these would gain better performance from the limited range of glass types available, but the practical problems were not overcome until the advent of computer-controlled machines in the late twentieth century. As vice-president of the society in 1678–80 he attended regularly; in January 1681 he

was elected president when Robert Boyle declined
the office, and he served for two years with energy
and distinction.

The Royal Society was also identified with Wren's
plan for rebuilding London immediately after the
great fire, for the problems of crowding, traffic,
smoke, and hygiene in a largely medieval city had
exercised fellows in the early 1660s. Within a fort-
night several plans were made; Wren's promptness
reflects his capacity for rapid thought. An ideal
plan and a document for discussion, the failure to
implement it has been lamented ever since, but its
completely new street pattern would have taken
too long, and cost too much, when the revival
of trade and commerce depended on the utmost
speed. His real part in the rebuilding was less spec-
tacular. As the most distinguished of the surveyors
chosen by crown and City soon after the fire to
deal with practical problems, he helped frame the
1667 and 1670 London Building Acts, whose pre-
cautionary regulations transformed the fabric of
the City; the most significant was the prohibition
of timber construction. As royal surveyor his first

task was the new custom house in Thames Street (1669–71, rebuilt 1718). With an eye to recent Dutch commercial architecture he made a warehouse resemble a royal palace—appropriately for a building representing the crown within a city jealous of its independence.

The case of Temple Bar (1670–72) is similar. To compel the City to rebuild its ceremonial western entrance, the king arranged for the money to be provided, his surveyor naturally producing the design. Wren's authorship is not documented, but his son claimed to have his original design, and once again its form is without precedent in city gateways. Temple Bar was re-erected at Theobalds Park, Hertfordshire, in 1878, and reconstructed in Paternoster Square, near St Paul's, in 2004. Otherwise Wren's creativity was severely limited by the state of the economy. The fire affected the whole nation, and work on the new Greenwich Palace designed by John Webb had been abandoned. Most of Wren's alterations to Hampton Court in the 1670s were swept away by William and Mary, while the constant additions at Whitehall, where rebuilding was also deferred, perished in the fires of 1691 and 1698. His principal work was administrative, but any doubt of his fitness, although relatively inexperienced, to rebuild the churches and cathedral would have been forestalled by his official position.

The City churches
and St Paul's

Church architect

A cathedral was so large and costly that neither
its commencement nor its completion could be
hurried, but on 17 May 1670 Wren took charge
of a small office, modelled on the office of
works, under the commissioners for rebuilding the
churches. He was responsible for about fifty new
churches in place of the eighty-six destroyed or
severely damaged in the fire; the total remains
inexact because, where a church only needed
repairs, his office merely handled the payments,
funded by a tax on all coal coming into London.
Moreover, St Clement Danes (a rebuilding) and
St Anne's, Soho, and St James's, Piccadilly (new
parishes), are in Westminster and unconnected

with the fire but are usually included. Wren's friends among the clergy were aware of new, mainly foreign, ideas about new types of building for protestant liturgy, but post-Reformation England was well provided with churches, even if many were run down. In the few seventeenth-century commissions new ideas had seldom been taken up, and the fire offered the opportunity of building specifically for the liturgy of the 1662 Book of Common Prayer and at the same time for proclaiming the reformed faith in a modern—classical—style of architecture.

Four decades later another building programme opened. Wren wrote a paper of advice for the Fifty New Churches Commission (1711) expounding his ideas in the light of experience, and exemplifying many of them by the paragon of St James's, Piccadilly. This was an 'auditory', of basilican plan but on similar principles to the Sheldonian Theatre. All should be able to see and hear clearly both the preacher in the pulpit and the celebrant at the communion table, which should be decorously but not dramatically emphasized.

Internal supports are few and slender. Large clear-glass windows give ample light, and galleries on three sides increase the accommodation. Wren's larger churches, on open sites, fit this general pattern though no two are identical. Other sites were far from ideal—small, irregular, cramped by secular neighbours. Some smaller churches are simple halls, rectangular or nearly rectangular (St Edmund the King, Lombard Street); often old foundations were reused at the expense of geometrical purity. Others have a single side aisle, sometimes with a gallery (St Margaret, Lothbury). Difficult sites spurred Wren's inventiveness: two churches were polygonal with oval domes of timber and plaster (St Benet Fink, Threadneedle Street, destroyed). Four others had round domes (for example St Mary Abchurch) and another four derive from a Byzantine type known to Wren by repute and used in the protestant Netherlands; in this, the arms of a Greek cross are defined within a square by four large columns (as in St Martin Ludgate). One of the finest churches, the most complex spatially and the purest geometrically, is St Stephen Walbrook, in which a dome coincides with the centre of a short Latin cross contained within a rectangle.

Building began in 1670–71 with fifteen churches; the rest followed, in batches or singly, until 1686, and most were completed by 1690 except for the elegant steeples that gave the city skyline its character until the early twentieth century. Most of these were added to finished towers in the twenty years after the renewal of the coal tax in 1697. Renaissance architects had consistently sought to adapt the steeple, a Gothic form, to the less emphatically vertical language of classicism. Wren completed one big London steeple, at St Mary-le-Bow, in 1680, providing not only an exemplar for the next two centuries but also a sample of what, when funds allowed, could be achieved in London.

One mind may invent many variations on a theme, but their execution would overburden even an architect otherwise uncommitted. Wren relied not only on administrators and draughtsmen but also on other designers. By

1670 Robert Hooke had taken up architecture, and in the main building campaign of the 1670s and 1680s was effectively in charge of several churches and was certainly a designer rather than a mere draughtsman. His diary from 1672 to 1680 shows them working so closely together, if not always harmoniously, that Hooke must be seen as Wren's associate. While an autograph Wren drawing may establish his sole authorship of a design, the evidence of Hooke's drawings is not in itself conclusive; Hooke's elevation for St Edmund the King, Lombard Street, bears Wren's initials as a mark of approval. Stylistic arguments are of limited value, even when not coloured by modern aesthetic criteria or the assumption that Wren was the better, more meticulous, or more 'advanced' partner. Nicholas Hawksmoor rose through the churches office from 1684 to 1701 and was designing by the early 1690s, but his creative share is elusive; his drawings for the lantern spire of St Augustine by St Paul, Watling Street, do not correspond to the building, and the last Wren steeples (St Vedast, St Stephen Walbrook) are very different from Hawksmoor's first designs under the 1711 New Churches Act. Similar doubt surrounds the contribution of William Dickinson in the office from 1691 onwards. Fittings and furniture of the churches were outside the commission's responsibility, paid for by individual parishes and designed by the executant craftsmen.

Wren's churches well suited the liturgy and the society of their time; this is evidenced by their influence on English religious architecture of the eighteenth and nineteenth centuries. But by about 1840 many were in poor repair and increasingly unsuited to changes in taste and liturgy. Moreover, as the City of London became a place only of work, not of residence, churches became redundant and their sites more valuable than their fabrics. The ecclesiological movement led to refurbishment: high box pews were removed, stalls were introduced for robed choirs before the altar, and stained glass was inserted. The progressive damage of these changes was exceeded by the effects of the Second World War, after which only half the churches were left and almost half of those had to be virtually rebuilt, often with further liturgical and decorative changes. Thus St Bride's, Fleet Street, was reseated as a sumptuous collegiate chapel, and the least altered survivors have, like St Peter Cornhill, largely Victorian interiors. The concept of 'a Wren church' has changed profoundly since his time, but the remaining examples are among the best-known and most popular of his works.

Designing a new cathedral

St Paul's has always been the touchstone of Wren's reputation. His association with it spans his whole architectural career, including the thirty-six years between the start of the new building in 1675 and the declaration by parliament of its completion in 1711. His first advice to the king in the autumn of 1661 was no doubt in consultation with the dean, John Barwick. Besides restoring services and repairing the Commonwealth damage and desecration, they envisaged completing the programme begun thirty years earlier by Inigo Jones for Charles I but abandoned in 1642 after the external recasing of the nave and transepts and the construction of a colossal western portico. A royal commission was opened on 18 April 1663; the surveyor, Sir John Denham, was a member; Wren was not, but was consulted. Among the clergy the driving force would be William Sancroft, dean after Barwick, from late 1664 to 1677. Subscriptions were invited and some work was done, but the fabric was obviously decrepit; the central tower, robbed of its wooden spire by lightning in 1567, was hazardous. Sancroft's second year in office was overshadowed by the plague, but on 1 May 1666 Wren, fresh from Paris, made a radical proposal, to replace the old crossing with four massive piers carrying a lofty dome, as 'an Ornament to His Majestie's most excellent Reign, to the Church of England, and to the great Citie' (Bolton and Hendry, 13.17). Within days he was preparing 'lines not discourses', and on 5 August he told Sancroft his drawings were finished; they extended Jones's 'trew latine' recasing to the interior of the Norman nave. At a site meeting on 27 August his design had a mixed reception, but Evelyn noted the cupola, 'a forme of Church-building

not as yet known in England, but of won-
derful grace' (*Diary*, 1955, 3.449). For Wren the
dome would be the most enduring legacy of his
travels. A week later the old cathedral was in
flames.

On 26 February 1667 Wren reported on the fea-
sibility of a temporary church in the ruins; on
15 January 1668 a makeshift choir and 'auditory' were ordered in the west end. Preparations
began, but Wren was scarcely surprised at Sancroft's letter of 25 April: 'What you whispered in
my Ear . . . is now come to pass. Our Work at the
West-end . . . is fallen about our Ears' (Bolton and
Hendry, 13.46). By July 1668 the commission had
requested a new design for 'a Quire, at least' (ibid.,
23), the king had ordered the demolition of the
old choir and crossing, and Sancroft told Wren to
'take it for granted, that Money will be had' (ibid.,
49).

Wren now envisaged a cruciform church on the
scale and orientation of the old one; the surviving plan (Wren drawings, All Souls College,

Oxford, II.42) retains the traditional long nave of medieval cathedrals, with a large dome at the crossing and a re-creation of Jones's portico. The detailing is classical: 'trew latine'. Progress was slow; appointed surveyor of repairs in succession to Denham on 30 July 1669, Wren could make no confident forecasts while funding was hypothetical and the site covered by ruins and rubble. After trying gunpowder to bring down large masses, he settled for a safer battering ram on the ancient Roman pattern.

The situation was considerably clearer by April 1670, when the distribution of coal tax revenue was extended to include St Paul's; Wren had, in anticipation, made a new design. Part of a wooden model survives at St Paul's, showing a galleried 'auditory' prefiguring St James's, Piccadilly, but twice as long and having, instead of side aisles under the galleries, arcades closed to the interior and open to the churchyard. Contemporary evidence of the missing part of the model is inadequate, but it certainly comprised a large and distinct western vestibule facing Ludgate Hill, which made the whole 'capable of any grand ceremony' (Wren, 282) and rose into a dome. This satisfied both the liturgical requirements and Wren's insistence on a noble modern city landmark; smaller and more compact than the old church, it reconciled parsimony with grandeur. The response was equivocal; some saw it as too novel and some as unimpressive. Not for the first or the last time, Wren wiped the slate clean. 'The generality', wrote his son, 'were for grandeur' (ibid.), and in March 1672 Wren was paid for drawings identifiably of an enormous domed Greek cross—basically a central mass carried on eight arches and ringed by an ambulatory. This costly and liturgically impractical late example of the ideal Renaissance centrally planned church would have set London to rival Paris or Rome; in November 1672 it received royal approval and a second model was ordered. But Wren constantly outpaced his paymasters, and within weeks he redesigned the whole building, adding a smaller domed western vestibule and a giant portico. On 12 November 1673 a new commission was opened; construction of the Great Model, still at St Paul's, was authorized as a record, and Wren was formally appointed surveyor to build the new cathedral rather than repair the old. Two days later he was knighted at Whitehall.

On 21 February 1674 Hooke walked through the Great Model; even undecorated, this object 6.3 metres long said more than drawings could about Wren's design. With a king prevaricating on the doorstep of Rome, the popish associations of a design so obviously emulating St Peter's were patent to those clergy desiring a traditional 'cathedral form'; moreover, it had an economic drawback. Medieval cathedrals were built in stages, starting with the choir or eastern arm, but a structure reducible to a dome with its supports must be erected—and funded—to completion before it was usable. Wren was confined to a 'cathedral form', albeit one closer to recent French basilican churches than to native Gothic prototypes: however, the warrant design, so called from the royal warrant of 14 May 1675 attached to the drawings (Wren drawings, All Souls College, Oxford,

II.9–14), is not the design on which work began only a few weeks later.

The building of St Paul's

Bureaucracy moves slowly, and from subsequent events it is clear that Wren both overhauled the Great Model even before its completion and also reworked the warrant design while the drawings awaited approval at Whitehall. This extraordinary conduct can only be understood in the knowledge that he had the confidence of Sancroft and of the king. The warrant design was the first to rest on an adequate brief: a traditional Latin cross plan, external elevations and portico re-creating Inigo Jones's, and the internal dome and exterior landmark now accepted as essential. But according to *Parentalia* Wren resolved to make no more models, which wasted time and aroused contention, nor to 'publickly expose his drawings' (Wren, 283). He also secured the king's privy licence for 'variations, rather ornamental than essential' (ibid.). The dome centre had been set out on site for the Great Model in the summer of 1673, and there was no formal foundation ceremony. Contemporaries record that an unidentified 'first stone' was placed in the footings on or about 21 June 1675; a month later the masons' contracts were completed and mains water supplied. Surviving preparatory drawings show Wren stretching to the limit the king's licence in a radical revision of the warrant design. This process occupied months before building started; when the design was complete it was, except for changes in detailing, final up to the roof-line. The drawings were known to very few; simple part-models and templates were used to guide the workmen. So effective was the secrecy that for years the London printmakers could offer only fictitious images of the new building, unaware that almost every dimension of the warrant design was changed and almost every feature of the exterior. The basilican elevation was replaced by two full storeys, rising clear of all other buildings more like a palace than a church, with a massive construction of thick walls and hidden flying buttresses to support adequately, both structurally and visually, a larger dome than proposed before the fire. Building proceeded from east to west, although for statical reasons all the crossing piers were carried on equally.

By 1694 the choir was ready for fitting; the first service was held there on 2 December 1697. By 1700 the body of the church was complete and the cylindrical base of the dome was rising. Engravings authorized in 1702 show a dome different both from that proposed in 1675 and from that finalized in 1704 when the western towers also were redesigned. There were financial as well as artistic reasons for the delay. Only the renewal of the coal tax in 1697 assured the worthy completion of the building, and with it the skyline that would dominate the City for the next two and a half centuries; the pure geometry of the dome deliberately contrasts with the complex western towers and the dozens of elaborate stone or leaded church steeples of which the last were finished in 1717. The last stone of the lantern was placed on 26 October 1708 by Wren's son Christopher, and by the end of the year the gilded ball and cross were in place.

The top of the cross is 111.5 metres above street level, only a few metres higher than the pre-fire design. Indeed most of the significant levels are very similar between Wren's first and last designs, but the last is much larger in diameter and in bulk and far more complex in structure. The inner dome, of brick, springs from a tapering drum containing large windows that flood in light, and terminates in an eye through which the inside of the lantern is visible. The outer dome, 16 metres higher and of lead-covered wood, provides a landmark visible from far and near without making the inside disproportionately lofty. This structure is carried by a brick cone springing from the same level as the inner dome and carrying the tall stone lantern that stabilizes the whole structure; the cone is invisible inside and outside. Both structurally and visually, Wren's dome is without identifiable precedent, but not surprisingly it has always been a source of wonder and an inspiration to many later architects.

The cathedral was declared complete in 1711, and Wren was paid the half of his salary that, in the misguided hope of accelerating progress, parliament had withheld for fourteen years. He did not attend the building commission after 1710; now in his late seventies, he faced accusations of condoning fraud and irregularity. Just as in earlier life he had been reluctant to offer full proof of the self-evident, he later cut corners in administration. Nothing was proved, but against his wishes the commission engaged Sir James Thornhill to paint the inner dome in false perspective, and finally in 1717 authorized a balustrade around the roof-line. This diluted the hard edge Wren had intended for his cathedral, and elicited the apt parthian comment that 'ladies think nothing well without an edging' (Bolton and Hendry, 16.131).

St Paul's is Wren's masterpiece; nevertheless it has always received adverse criticism, much of it for not fitting the critic's idea of a post-medieval protestant cathedral. History has inevitably brought change. Especially since the Second World War building heights have risen, and the cathedral no longer stands proud of its neighbours. Yet open planning has given better views of the building as a whole than Wren ever expected, designing for a constricted site virtually rebuilt before work started, on the building lines of a medieval city such as Rouen or Florence. Within, Wren had minimized the apparent length of the nave, turning the western bays into a broad assembly area and obscuring the west–east vista by a wooden organ screen between the dome area and the choir. Until well into the nineteenth century all services were held in the choir and the rest of the building was unseated; thereafter urban expansion and the vogue for theatrical sermons led to the removal of the screen, the division of the organ, and the effect of a single continuous space amply seated. The persistent desire of artists to embellish Wren's white light-filled interior finally resulted, at the end of the nineteenth century, in the mosaic treatment of the choir vaults and successive attempts to provide a grander setting for the altar.

A public architect

Secular work of the 1670s

During the 1670s Wren received significant secular commissions which manifest both the maturity and the variety of his architecture and the sensitivity of his response to diverse briefs; two of these works also involved Robert Hooke. The Monument commemorating the great fire, erected on Fish Street Hill near its source, was funded from the coal tax (1671–6). It is a colossal column, a concept consciously indebted to Roman models; several projects survive from different hands, including Hooke's. Wren was certainly in control of the final design, which is not Hooke's— an orthodox fluted Doric column, probably modelled on the smaller one erected in Paris a century earlier for Catherine de' Medici. For the apex Wren proposed a colossal statue of Charles II, but the king preferred the striking symbol of a flaming urn in gilt bronze to the imperial associations of a statue.

Hooke also worked on the Royal Observatory on the hill above the palace (and later Royal Naval Hospital) at Greenwich. It was built rapidly in 1675–6 for John Flamsteed, the astronomer royal, to make a new star map in the hope of solving the problem of longitude in navigation. Half a century later the problem was solved with John Harrison's clock, but the observatory site, chosen by Wren, gave the world Greenwich mean time and the zero meridian. The site offered height and clear air away from London, and the firm base of Duke Humphrey's Tower, a derelict fort; construction was therefore directed not by the king's works but by the Board of Ordnance. It was a rural building designed to a low budget, little more than the £500 offered by the king. It recalls the conceits—and the specifically English 'Renaissance' style—of Elizabeth's reign. The lead-capped turrets answer those of the Tower, the headquarters of the Ordnance a few miles upriver, and the tall windows of the great octagonal room accommodated long telescope tubes—at least until the equipment outgrew the room and its floor proved shakier than the foundation below. Although much of the management was Hooke's, it is simplistic to imagine that Wren, personally engaged by the king, relinquished control of a design he had many reasons to foster.

The library of Trinity College, Cambridge, was entirely in Wren's hands although directed from London. It is his most elegant building and the grandest library in Cambridge. His drawings and an accompanying letter (Wren drawings, All Souls College, Oxford, I.44–7) illuminate his design in exceptional detail. It is a traditional European collegiate library—a long upper room above a cloister walk—but it is much more. Wren's colleague Isaac Barrow, master of Trinity, having failed to interest his university in a 'theatre' or Senate House like Sheldon's in Oxford, with an added library, decided to improve his own college, whose library had suffered a serious fire. A new site was available: the open river end of Nevile's Court, whose sides comprised ranges of lodgings with ground-level arcades. There was space for a magnificent building that would attract gifts of books and money, and Wren's first proposal was for a free-standing circular domed reading room shelved around the perimeter wall—an idea before its time, and only practicable on the scale of Sir Anthony Panizzi's British Museum Library.

The preferred solution appeared more conventional, continuing the old cloister walk and upper-floor level across the opening. However, in most respects the new building differs from its neighbours. It is larger in scale and visually distinct on both sides. Decoration is sparing and scrupulously classical. But while the court front is open and articulated by arches and half-columns, the back is closed, astylar, and entirely rectilinear, exemplifying Wren's opinion in one of his tracts that things not visible together need not correspond. This also applies to the interior, even less predictable from without than the Sheldonian or the first model for St Paul's. In fact, like the executed dome of the cathedral, Trinity Library consists of disparate exterior and interior linked by an unseen common structure. The cloister walk is low, limited by the continuous floor level overhead, and the library interior is twice as high, allowing a zone for bookcases with a range of tall windows above it; yet the external elevations appear to be two equal storeys.

The discrepancy is resolved by a remarkable integrated and consistent physical structure. With a logic worthy of twentieth-century frame building, a regular system of supports rises from foundations through piers to transverse beams and book-stacks and to windows and roof trusses. This powerful hidden geometry conditions visible and sensible experience of the building; it dictates where the bookcases stand and is expressed even in the compartmented ceiling Wren intended, added only in 1850–51. Wren's letter to Barrow explains his choice of flooring for quietness and comfort, considerations as important as his conscious imitation in the cloister walk of the Greek *stoa* and his rejection of an exterior giant order of pillars as over-scale. Other features were hidden until repair works revealed them in the 1920s: inverted arches in the foundations, complex floor beams carrying the book-stacks, and iron tie-rods within them. The span of Wren's career saw changes in English architecture comparable to almost three centuries in Renaissance Italy, and in this development Trinity Library is closest to the High Renaissance of Donato Bramante and Jacopo Sansovino.

Domestic and public life

Wren's domestic life is best documented in the 1670s, partly because the major portion (1672–80) of Hooke's diary records—albeit briefly—their frequent conversations. These concerned not only the new churches and cathedral but many other matters. This period also encompassed most of Wren's married life. Gilbert, the first child of Wren and Faith, was baptized on 26 October 1672 and buried on 23 March 1674; their second, Christopher, was born on 18 February 1675. Faith died on 3 September 1675, of smallpox. On

24 February 1677 Wren married Jane (1639?–1680), the daughter of William, second Baron Fitzwilliam of Lifford, at the Chapel Royal (probably Whitehall), of which Wren's brother-in-law Holder was subdean. The private ceremony may have been precipitate; it surprised Hooke, and a daughter, Jane, was baptized on 13 November. William was born on 16 June 1679. His mother died on 4 October 1680, leaving the architect with three small children; their ties remained close, so it is reasonable to suppose that they were brought up at Scotland Yard. Until 1687, when her husband left the Chapel Royal, Wren's sister Susan Holder was a neighbour; their own mother had died early, she had helped to bring up Christopher, and now she probably helped with his children. Another member of the household throughout the 1680s was the young Nicholas Hawksmoor, Wren's personal assistant and most talented informal pupil.

Wren never went abroad after 1666, and in 1698 he advised his son Christopher against going on aimlessly from France to Italy. The king's business took him on occasion to Dover, Newmarket,

Hampton Court, Windsor, Portland, Winchester, and elsewhere, but he preferred clients and even artificers to visit him in London, within reach of most of his work. From Scotland Yard he could reach St Paul's in under half an hour on foot—less by river—and there is no good evidence that he ever lived elsewhere. He would go to the City several times a week, reserving Saturdays for St Paul's; in Paris he had noted with approval the weekly inspections of the Louvre works by Colbert, the king's superintendent of buildings. Wren's daughter Jane died unmarried on 29 December 1702 and was buried at St Paul's; according to her monument there, she was talented in letters and music, lived at home, and was greatly mourned. William was disabled; in 1698 his father called him 'poor Billy ... lost to me and to the world' (Bolton and Hendry, 19.119), but he lived until 15 March 1738, his father's will having provided for his care.

'Architecture has its political use', Wren wrote, and he seems to have considered himself a public architect (Wren, 351). Although his priorities were his buildings and his family, he occasionally engaged energetically in other areas. Between 1679 and 1683 he sat on the committee of the Hudson's Bay Company, in which he had bought stock. His family's politics appear to have been conservative, just as their religion was orthodox. He nevertheless stood for parliament several times, failing election for Cambridge University in March 1667 and for Oxford in January 1674. In James II's parliament he represented Plympton St Maurice, Devon, from 1685 to July 1687 and was active in committee work; his motive in this instance was probably to secure continued funding for St Paul's. In 1689–90 he was twice elected for New Windsor, but both elections were overturned. From late in 1701 until the death of William III the following March he represented Melcombe Regis.

Wren's opinion was also sought on monetary reform. In 1695 he reported, with others, on the coinage (Ming-Hsun Li, *The Great Recoinage of 1696 to 1699*, London, 1963, appx 1). His shrewd assessment of the problems included cogent and practical arguments for a new standard coin divided centesimally, an idea proposed by Robert Wood in the 1650s.

Royal works of the 1680s

By historical accident all Wren's large secular commissions date from after 1680. At the age of fifty his personal development, as was that of English architecture, was ready for a monumental but humane architecture, in which the scale of individual parts related both to the whole and to the people who used them. Wren's first essay, the Chelsea Hospital, does not entirely satisfy the eye in this respect, but met its brief with such distinction and success that even in the twenty-first century it fulfils its original function, albeit with the benefit of modern standards of comfort and hygiene. The project stemmed from concern for the veterans of civil war armies and the new regiments instituted by Charles II. Most of the funding came from subscriptions and from a levy on soldiers' pay. Wren asked no fee for his design, the main bulk of which was built by 1685, with

extensions under James II and William III. However, on completion in 1693 a gratuity acknowledged his responsibility for the work.

Chelsea offered the standards of light and venti-
lation recently set by Hooke's Bethlem Hospital;
it also deliberately emulated—more in concept
than design—the Invalides of Louis XIV, plans of
which reached Whitehall in 1678. Both king and
architect recognized the 'political use' and propa-
ganda value of the building, not only to house
several hundred pensioned soldiers but also to
display the magnanimity of the king. The wards
at Chelsea are partitioned to give individual pri-
vacy while keeping the camaraderie of regimental
life; here, as in any domestic building, the standard door and window are the units of scale. But
the size of the central court, a rectangle of some
70 metres, and the building's symbolism, warrant the giant columns and pilasters in the centre
of each elevation. In places the two scales come
into conflict; Wren, who habitually stated rather
than argued a case, must have been satisfied with
this.

The new palace begun in 1683 at Winchester, the ancient capital of England, was similar in scale and prestige. Winchester was near the coast and far from the eye of Westminster, and the narrowing sequence of courts imitates that of Versailles, still being enlarged for Louis XIV. Both king and surveyor understood the ironic compliment to Louis; Charles received secret subsidies from the latter in return for promises, subsequently broken. Work stopped on Charles's death in 1685; ultimately converted into barracks, the building was gutted in 1894 and replaced by a historicist pastiche. Imperfect images of the original suffice to show that, with time, Wren had absorbed the impact of Bernini's project for the Louvre, drawings of which, in 1665, he 'would have given my skin for' (Wren, 262): a flat balustraded skyline replaced the pitched roofs and dormers he had used at Chelsea, and a square mansard dome was to crown the porticoed centre.

King Charles's reconstruction of the state rooms at Windsor Castle was notable for the integration of architecture, sculpture, and illusionist painting, a style long identified by scholars as a hallmark of the European baroque and the favourite of absolutist rulers. These works were in the hands of a separate comptroller, Hugh May, and were virtually complete when, on May's death in February 1684, Wren assumed his post and seems to have persuaded the Treasury that May's Whitehall comptrollership was superfluous, until the appointment by William and Mary of William Talman in May 1689. His first commission in this genre was therefore the new Roman Catholic chapel at Whitehall Palace, part of a new range ordered by James II soon after his accession. The interior, fulsomely described by Evelyn upon its opening in December 1686, was burnt down in January 1698 with most of the palace, including the highly decorated riverside apartments and the terrace Wren began in 1688 for Mary of Modena and finished for Mary II.

Commissions under William and Mary

Wren's only palace to be both completed and preserved is therefore Hampton Court. In 1687 he had feared for his post under James II's policy of appointing Roman Catholics, but he survived both this and the revolution of 1688. William and Mary visited Hampton Court within days of their accession in February 1689 and found it old-fashioned but attractive. A new home nearer London was also necessary, since William refused to live in damp and smoke-ridden Whitehall. By midsummer, work was in progress on partly rebuilding Hampton Court, and the sovereigns had bought a Jacobean mansion near Kensington village from the earl of Nottingham. Wren was in charge both of Hampton Court and of transforming Nottingham House into Kensington Palace. Both works were, like Chelsea and Winchester, brick built with stone dressings. In an Anglophile monarch this was not from Dutch taste but from economy, the shortage of masons and Portland stone during the building of St Paul's, and—not least—the king's desire for speed, which led William to take some responsibility for a fall of masonry at Kensington; after a more serious accident at Hampton Court, he supported Wren against efforts by

the new comptroller, Talman, to discredit
him.

Between February and June 1689 Wren drew several designs for Hampton Court, reducing a vast palace, retaining only the Tudor great hall, to new south and east ranges housing the king's and queen's apartments and suggesting to the traveller from London a square block rivalling the centre of Versailles. This compromise preserved the extensive Tudor kitchens and other service buildings, and the new structure was finished when Mary died at the end of 1694. Work then ceased until the treaty of Ryswick (September 1697) released William from the European wars. The exterior of Hampton Court has been faulted by purists misinterpreting Wren's empirical skill in providing the essentials of a modern palace with speed and economy. He was now master of large-scale civil architecture, and both the richness of colour, texture, and imagery and the convincing illusion of a great four-storey block almost 100 metres square show the continuing attraction of Versailles. During his last year William held court at rural Hampton in emulation of the French palace. With the loss of Whitehall and most of Stuart Windsor, Hampton Court has the only surviving state suites of the period; however, Wren's designs of 1694 were discarded, and Talman was probably responsible for the interiors of the King's Side; the Queen's Side was finished for Queen Anne.

At Kensington between 1689 and 1696 Wren, assisted by Hawksmoor as clerk of works, rebuilt much of the house, inserting state rooms and adding service ranges. By 1718, when George I commissioned further state rooms replacing the core of the old house, Wren was virtually powerless in the works. Three centuries later Kensington Palace is still a suburban mansion set in extensive gardens. Wren's greatest secular work would have been an entirely new Whitehall, but as imaginative artefacts his large drawings for two alternative projects (now at All Souls, Oxford) have a place in his work analogous to the Great Model. The fire of 1691 destroyed the south end of the riverside range, but on 4 January

1698 a more serious fire reduced the rambling Tudor palace and the many seventeenth-century additions to rubble and ashes; little remained beyond the buildings facing St James's Park and Inigo Jones's Banqueting House, whose protection Wren had ordered at all costs. His new designs gave prominence to the latter; besides its intrinsic merits it was remembered—if not always honoured—as the execution place of Charles I. Wren must have made his designs very soon after the fire: King William saw status but no use in a palace there, and his deferment to parliament of financial provision effectively ended the project. The dream of a great metropolitan palace of linked courts had been sustained by impecunious monarchs and their surveyors since Charles I and Jones; Wren succeeded in managing such large and complex masses, using both giant and smaller columns, and varied rhythms, scales, and textures. The larger components offered strong relief and richness of shadow; the progression through the courts would have been as exciting as the sheer size of individual units. With an idiosyncratic freedom of vocabulary born of long experience, Wren's Whitehall would have stood comparison with contemporary continental palaces, occupying the place in civil architecture he had foreseen for his cathedral in religious.

Mechanical hand and philosophical mind

The Royal Naval Hospital, Greenwich

Wren's response to a challenge is nowhere better seen than in his last major building, the Royal Naval Hospital at Greenwich. The sea victory of La Hogue (1692) cost serious casualties, a number of whom were accommodated in the abandoned palace begun for Charles II by John Webb in 1664. The philanthropic concerns underlying Chelsea turned to the navy, and Wren was among those who in 1693 discussed a permanent institution on this site. The sovereigns' grant of the site in October 1694 stemmed from Queen Mary's particular interest and her desire for greater magnificence than Chelsea's. Wren again gave his services free; however, Nicholas Hawksmoor was paid as his personal clerk from 1696, thereafter as clerk of works, and, in 1705, as Wren's deputy. Work began in 1696 on completing and converting Webb's building, with a service range behind it.

Wren made several designs before producing his final one early in 1698. His brief was constrained by the extent and nature of the site, bounded on the north by the Thames and on the west by the area around Webb's building. In the park to the south lay Inigo Jones's Queen's House. Webb had envisaged a large court open to the river, its sides formed by his original building on the west and a duplicate on the east; the axis of the court was in line with the Queen's House, but he proposed to block it with a third building with a domed centrepiece. Wren explored this theme, although he already knew that this axis was excluded from the royal gift and could not be built upon. Seen from the river, the customary approach, Greenwich is thus a building without a middle, but Wren exploited this defect by treating the whole like a classical landscape, with tall domed vestibules framing the house and the hill behind it. In the foreground he duplicated Webb's building as originally intended, and in the middle distance the domes mark the nearer and inner corners of courtyards containing hall, chapel, and ward blocks. The proscribed land is framed by receding colonnades, a form which, he observed, could extend to any length without disproportion. The appearance of the observatory several degrees off the axis—a flaw to eighteenth-century eyes—picturesquely softens the formal symmetry of the newer buildings.

After brief euphoria funds failed, and the hospital took almost a century to complete. Wren's vision was realized as far as the setting and layout and almost everything visible on the main axis are concerned; elsewhere other and later designers contributed. Almost from the start Hawksmoor had a free hand in the courts behind the colonnades, and the western one (1698–1704) is largely his, including the detailing of the great hall painted by Sir James Thornhill. Neither Wren nor Hawksmoor designed the later eastern court, including the chapel. The hospital was in use until 1869 and reopened four years later as the Royal Naval College. In 1997, as the buildings were transferred to civilian education, the outstanding character and beauty of Greenwich, including Wren's hospital, were recognized by designation as a UNESCO world heritage site.

Wren and Gothic: domestic work

In 1713 Wren wrote a surveyor's report on Westminster Abbey. Although medieval architecture, subsumed in the seventeenth century under the name Gothic, was generally disparaged in the prevailing Renaissance aesthetic, the royal architect was inevitably involved in the care of historic buildings. In churches and the universities the tradition of the pointed arch had not quite died out when the fashion for conscious medievalism began that led to the Gothic revival. Wren was prepared to admire in private ancient buildings disparaged by his public taste. In an earlier report on Salisbury Cathedral (1668) he commended the structural audacity—rather than skill—of the medieval builder, but also appreciated the beauty of its illumination and the simplicity of its window tracery. Even before the fire he meant to modernize St Paul's. The Westminster report, however, is clear that repairing or completing Gothic buildings requires a historically sympathetic eye. In 1698 he succeeded Hooke as surveyor of a Westminster with its west front and towers still unfinished and the crossing unmarked externally. His part in the long-term building programme was largely by delegation to William Dickinson; the completion of the west end was due to Hawksmoor in the 1730s. The 1713 report illustrates Wren's theoretical position. He had been obliged in some of the City churches 'to deviate from a better style'; the obvious but controversial example is St Mary Aldermary (1679–82), which was funded from a private bequest. Some old materials were used, but archaeology has established that it is not the simple reconstruction of a Tudor building it appears to be. The unique plaster fan vaults have more in common with archaistic seventeenth-century vaults in Oxford (as in Brasenose College chapel, 1659) than with

Tudor ones. In the same years and style Wren designed Tom Tower, the belfry completing the gateway to Christ Church, Oxford.

Wren had no connection with the popular concept of the 'Wren house', a rectangular gentry house with a hipped roof invented before the civil war and fashionable beyond the seventeenth century. There is substantial evidence for his authorship of two plain but elegant houses, designed for Whitehall colleagues and successive Treasury ministers: Tring Manor, Hertfordshire, for Henry Guy, and Winslow Hall, Buckinghamshire, for William Lowndes. In both the interior disposition is unusual but logical. Tring (c.1687–90) was remodelled in the 1870s, but the carcase survives, including the dramatic arrangement of stair hall and two-storey great room along the middle of the house. Roger North, who knew architect and client, attests Wren's authorship. Winslow (1699–1702) is little altered, a three-storey double pile with matching end staircases and a spine-wall containing the chimney flues. Wren was also engaged by the duchess

of Marlborough to design Marlborough House,
Pall Mall (1709–11, attic storeys added 1861–3).
He indeed carried responsibility for this, but
Colen Campbell ascribes the design to his son,
'Christopher Wren, Esq.' (*Vitruvius Britannicus*,
1, 1715, 5).

Wren's last years

The duchess had her plain brick house, but she
dismissed Wren with the interior unfinished.
Handwriting suggests a serious illness early in
1711; he recovered, but his immediate circle must
have been anxious to conceal his condition in the
face of mounting criticism of his competence and
his taste. Nevertheless both Wrens were appointed
to the Fifty New Churches Commission of October
1711, and Sir Christopher was an active member
during the first months when the commission
was framing its programme. The new commission of December 1715 included no architects. His
comprehensive letter of advice to his colleagues
(already mentioned) draws on his own experience
with the City churches.

Other attacks followed. In 1712 the *Letter Concerning Design* of Anthony Ashley Cooper, third earl of Shaftesbury, circulated in manuscript. Proposing a new British style of architecture (generally interpreted as neo-Palladianism), Shaftesbury censured Wren's cathedral, his taste, and his long-standing control of the royal works. In 1715 the surveyorship was put into commission, leaving Wren in nominal charge of a board of works. On 26 April 1718, on the pretext of failing powers, he was dismissed in favour of the incompetent William Benson. He left Scotland Yard for the Old Court House on Hampton Court Green, the official residence of which he had obtained a personal lease in 1708. In 1714 he had claimed to the Royal Society—prematurely—to have solved the longitude problem; the treatise he promised is lost.

Besides official and personal letters, Wren's surviving writings comprise occasional reports, his Gresham lecture, and five incomplete 'tracts' on the theory and history of architecture. These (reprinted by Soo, 1998) were transcribed by his son; with his church reports they provide the

principal evidence of his view of architecture. The
tracts, probably dating from early in his architectural career, may represent lectures or drafts
connected with the early Royal Society's publication programme. Wren's theory is empirical,
embracing both the certainties of natural (geometrical) law proclaimed in the Gresham lecture and the accidents of the world of experience.
While he discovered in architecture the grandest
of geometrical demonstrations, he acknowledged
the customary and arbitrary elements of the
observer's experience. If we experience his cathedral as geometry made real, that was his inten-
tion, but it has no numerical basis. For Wren the
authority of the classical orders and Vitruvius's
De architectura was no more absolute than that
of the Latin or Greek classics; nothing should be
accepted on the mere word of the ancients, and
every design should derive from first principles.
Thus Wren might use an earlier building as an
exemplar but would in no sense copy it, and more
of his detail is invented than derived. Especially
at St Paul's he developed drawing as a method of
design research, but he recognized that drawings,

models, and buildings appear differently to the eye.

Wren died on 25 February 1723 at his son's house in St James's Street, Westminster, after 'catching a cold' (Ward, 106); the attribution of this to a winter visit to St Paul's is apocryphal. He was buried on 5 March in the cathedral crypt, beneath a simple black marble floor slab. An inscribed wall-tablet nearby ends with the words *Si monumentum requiris, circumspice* ('If you seek his monument, look around you'). By either temperament or experience Wren was, according to his son, a 'Christian stoic'. Physically slight and sparing of words, he impressed all who met him.

Wren's achievement and reputation

Even if Wren had died in the great plague he would have merited biographical attention. The mathematician William Oughtred had called him at sixteen 'a youth of absolutely marvellous talent' (Wren, 184), and John Evelyn, at twenty-two, a 'miracle of a youth' (Evelyn, *Diary*, 3.106). In 1662

Isaac Barrow described him as 'once a prodigy of a boy; now, a miracle of a man, nay, even something divine' (Wren, 346). Three years later, in the preface to *Micrographia*, Robert Hooke wrote that 'Since the time of Archimedes, there scarce ever met in one man, in so great a perfection, such a Mechanical Hand, and so Philosophical a Mind.' Among several references to Wren in his *Principia* (1687), Isaac Newton not only called him 'one of the foremost geometers of this age' but acknowledged his prior formulation of the inverse-square law for the force governing the motion of the planets.

The fullest tribute to his early achievement is that of Thomas Sprat. Sprat, in a unique exception to his own rule, named Wren among fellows of the society, because many of his discoveries had gone unrecorded and some 'he did only start and design...since carry'd to perfection by the Industry of other hands'. Sprat continued, 'It is not Flattery but honesty, to give him his just praise; who is so far from usurping the fame of other men, that he indeavours with all care to conceal his own'

(*History of the Royal Society*, 1667, 317–18). By all accounts Wren's opinions and his habitually well-chosen words were valued. At the Royal Society on 21 June 1665 the subject of human flight was discussed, a topic of particular interest in the light of John Wilkins's recent speculations about flight both within and beyond our atmosphere (*Discovery of a New World*, 1640 edn). The meeting was concerned with the former, but Wren's comment showed his grasp of the mechanics involved and forestalled further speculation: 'a man would be able so often to move his wings, as he could with double his own weight on his back ascend a pair of stairs built at an angle of 45 degrees' (T. Birch, *History of the Royal Society*, 1776, 2.59).

Nevertheless contemporaries observed Wren's brilliance rather than his practical achievement. Even among the originals who founded the Royal Society, Wren was exceptional. He was younger than most; he published little. He did not adopt and monopolize one specialism; he discarded any problem he knew how to solve, and his attention span was short. Contemporaries complained that he valued the neatness of a solution above the presentation of proofs, claiming that the truth, once stated, was self-evident. Like his fellows he subscribed to Bacon's principle of the utility of the sciences, but he was not the archetypal Baconian that Sprat, the Royal Society's apologist, made him out to be. In his Gresham lecture and in his practical work he took a different course. While his motto, *Numero, pondere et mensura* ('Number, weight, and measure'), does not preclude scepticism, it looks towards the certainties of divine order, founded in the truths of number. His experimental work was by turns optical, mechanical, and physiological; it tended always towards highly visible results—lenses and optical images, machines, models, and dissections. Accumulations of statistical or observational data bored him. He relinquished the microscope, and his use of the telescope became occasional. As in the case of Pascal, he preferred geometrical, visual, and intuitive solutions for mathematical problems.

Wren was of his time, and any but the narrowest definition of English baroque must include him;

there are many parallels between his later work and that of Hardouin-Mansart, Carlo Fontana, and J. L. von Hildebrandt on the continent. As the architect of St Paul's and the City churches, Wren is England's most famous architect, but he has never fitted a stereotype. Criticisms of St Paul's have always been so diverse as to cancel each other; like all masterworks it changed perceptions of its genre. This was recognized in the praise (*Analysis of Beauty*, 1753) of William Hogarth, who shared not only Wren's respect for nature and empiricism in art but also his mingled understanding and distrust of the arts of France. Horace Walpole's praise is tempered by the observation that he had 'great ability, rather than taste' (Walpole, *Anecdotes of Painting in England*, 1849, 2.181). *Parentalia*'s emphasis on taste is deliberate; Wren, whose contemporaries were Bunyan, Dryden, and Pepys, was a Restoration, not a Georgian, figure. His genius has been seen in versatility, desire to succeed, survival to complete his cathedral. His English prose reflects the justness rather than the complexity of his school Latin. In architecture, perhaps as early as 1663, he reformulated for himself and the next generation classical 'Vitruvian' principles of architecture, as an empirical system of which his writings reveal only fragments but which informs all his designs. He fostered talent where he found it—Nicholas Hawksmoor is the outstanding example, following his teaching rather than his style—but the idiosyncrasy of his colleagues and the popularity of a new Palladian architecture based on rules of taste precluded the development of a 'Wren school'.

Wren's first biographer was not his son but the slightly younger John Ward (1740); James Elmes's centenary biography relies heavily on both Ward and *Parentalia*, and does justice to the scientific work, as did F. C. Penrose in the first edition of the *Dictionary of National Biography* (1900). At the close of the nineteenth century, the century of revivals, Wren was due for imitation, and the term 'Wrenaissance' was coined. A by-product of this interest was the establishment of the Wren Society, whose unique twenty-volume series published hundreds of drawings, documents, and other records of him and his associates. His science was neglected, but in 1937 John Summerson's essay *The Tyranny of Intellect* extended the mould formed by Sprat to present him as an artist hampered by the logic of a scientific mind. The deficiencies of this view have since become evident, and we can now see that Wren's brilliance lay in the unique breadth, depth, diversity, and consistency of his mind.

Sources

C. Wren, *Parentalia, or, Memoirs of the family of the Wrens* (1750) [facs. edn 1965] · A. T. Bolton and H. D. Hendry, eds., *The Wren Society*, 20 vols. (1924–43) · K. Downes, *The architecture of Wren*, 2nd edn (1988) · *The diary of Robert Hooke … 1672–1680*, ed. H. W. Robinson and W. Adams (1935) · B. Little, *Sir Christopher Wren: a historical biography* (1975) · J. Summerson, *Sir Christopher Wren* (1953) · J. Ward, *The lives of the professors of Gresham College* (1740) · J. Elmes, *Memoirs of the life and works of Sir Christopher Wren* (1823) · H. M. Colvin and others, *The history of the king's works*, 5 (1976) · A. N. L. Munby, ed., *Sale catalogues of libraries of eminent persons*, 4, ed. D. J. Watkin (1972), 1–43 · J. Summerson, 'The mind of Wren', *Heavenly mansions and other essays on architecture* (1949), 51–86 · J. A. Bennett, *The mathematical science of Christopher Wren* (1982) · M. Hunter, 'The making of Christopher Wren', *London Journal*, 16 (1991), 101–16 · K. Downes, *Sir Christopher Wren: the design of St Paul's* (1988) · K. Downes, *Sir Christopher Wren: an exhibition* (1982) [exhibition catalogue, Whitechapel Art Gallery, London, 9 July–26 Sept 1982] · *Aubrey's Brief lives*, ed. O. L. Dick (1949) · A. F. E. Poley, *St Paul's Cathedral measured, drawn and described*, 2nd edn (1932) · M. Feingold, 'The humanities', *The history of the University of Oxford*, 4: *Seventeenth-century Oxford*, ed. N. Tyacke (1997), 211–358 · M. Feingold, 'The mathematical sciences and new philosophies', *The history of the University of Oxford*, 4: *Seventeenth-century Oxford*, ed. N. Tyacke (1997), 359–448 · J. Summerson, 'The penultimate design for St Paul's', *Burlington Magazine*, 103 (1961), 83–9 · K. Downes, 'Sir Christopher Wren, Edward Woodroffe, J. H. Mansart and architectural history', *Architectural History*, 37 (1994), 37–67 · J. A. Bennett, 'Christopher Wren: the natural causes of beauty', *Architectural History*, 15 (1972), 5–22 · J. A. Bennett, 'A study of *Parentalia*', *Annals of Science*, 30 (1973), 129–47 · P. Jeffery, *The City churches of Sir Christopher Wren* (1996) · L. M. Soo, *Wren's 'tracts' on architecture and other writings* (1998) · D. McKitterick, ed., *The making of the Wren Library, Trinity College, Cambridge* (1995) · T. F. Reddaway, *The rebuilding of London after the great fire* (1940) · J. Bold, *Greenwich: an architectural history of the Royal Hospital for Seamen and the Queen's House* (2000) · M. Hunter, *Science and society in Restoration England* (1981) · R. G. Frank, *Harvey and the Oxford physiologists* (1980) · L. Weaver, *Sir Christopher Wren* (1923)

Index

A
Aristotle 6, 11–12
Aubrey, John 1–4

B
Bacon, Francis 7, 11–12, 81
Boyle, Robert 7, 8–9

C
Charles II 15–16, 20–1, 26–7,
        30, 44–5, 52–3, 57–8,
        60–3
Chelsea Hospital 60–1, 69
churches, rebuilding of
        London's 26–7, 31,
        33–9, 73, 75, 82
Coghill, Faith (wife) 28, 56–7

D
Denham, John 27, 40, 42

E
Emmanuel College,
        Cambridge, chapel and
        cloister at 25–6

E
Evelyn, John 7–8, 25, 40–1, 63,
        78

F
Fitzwilliam, Mary (wife) 57

G
George I 66
Gilbert, William 11
gothic architecture 72–5
great fire of London 26–31,
        51–2
Greenwich
    Royal Naval Hospital 69–72
    Royal Observatory 52–3

H
Hampton Court 30–1, 63–5
Hawksmoor, Nicholas 25,
        37–8, 57, 66, 69–73,
        83
Holder, Susan (née Wren)
        (daughter) 4, 57
Holder, William 3–6 , 57

Hooke, Robert 7, 16, 21, 37, 44, 51, 53, 56–7, 61, 73, 79

J
James II 61, 63, 64

K
Kensington Palace 64, 66

L
London, plans for rebuilding 29–30

M
Marlborough House, Pall Mall 74–5
Mary II 30–1, 63–5, 69
monetary reform 58–9
Monument, the (to the great fire of London) 51–2

N
'new philosophy', Wren's views on 10–12

P
Pascal, Blaise 13–14, 16, 81
Pembroke College, Cambridge, chapel at 22–3

R
Royal Naval Hospital, Greenwich 69–72
Royal Observatory, Greenwich 52–3
Royal Society 7, 15, 17, 21, 23–5, 28–9, 76–7, 79–81

S
Sancroft, William 40–1, 45
Sheldonian Theatre, Oxford 23, 34
Sprat, Thomas 7, 79–81, 84
St Jame's church, Piccadilly 33, 34–5
St Mary Aldermary church 73–4
St Mary-le-Bow church 36
St Paul's cathedral
    building of the new cathedral 39–50
    completion of 47–9
    criticism of 49–50, 76, 82
    designing the new cathedral 39–45, 55, 77–8, 82
    dome of cathedral 40–1, 43–8
    models for building 42–6
    repair and rebuilding of the old cathedral 16, 26–7, 33, 39–41
St Stephen Walbrook church 35–6

T
Temple Bar 30
Trinity College, Cambridge, library at 53–6

V
Vitruvius Pollio, Marcus 19, 20, 77, 83

W
Ward, Seth 7, 14
Webb, John 69–70

Westminster Abbey 72, 73
Whitehall Palace 27, 63, 66–8
Wilkins, John 6–9
William III 30–1, 61, 63–8
Winchester Palace 62
Windsor Castle, state rooms
        at 62–3
Winslow Hall,
        Buckinghamshire
        74–5
Wren, Christopher
    achievements 78–84
    All Soul's College, Oxford 7,
        14
    architect, Wren's career as
        an
        early commissions 22–6
        established architect,
            Wren as 26–31
        Gothic architecture 72–5
        first steps to becoming an
            architect 19–22
        royal works of
            1680s 60–3
        secular work of the
            1670s 51–6, 60–3
        tracts on 77
    astronomy, Wren's work
        in 8–15, 79
    biographies of Wren 83
    birth 1
    children 3, 4, 10, 14, 20, 45,
        47, 56–8, 67, 75–8, 82
    churches, rebuilding of
        London's 26–7, 31,
        33–9, 73, 75, 82
    criticism of 49–50, 65,
        75–6, 80–2
    death 78
    domestic life 56–8

    early life and education
        2–7
    Gresham College,
        London 9–14, 19
    Gresham inaugural lecture
        August 1657 10–13, 15,
        20, 76–7, 81
    last years 75–8
    marriage 28
    mathematics, work in 5,
        10–14, 16–17, 81
    member of parliament,
        Wren as 59
    monetary reform 59–60
    'new philosophy', Wren's
        views of the 10–12
    optics, work in 8–9, 15–17,
        28, 81
    Paris, travel to 21–2, 58
    reputation 13–17, 78–84
    royal works of 1680s 60–3
    Savilian chair of astronomy
        at Oxford, election
        to 14–15, 16–17
    scientific work 6–15, 28–9,
        84
    Scotland Yard, residence
        at 28, 57–8, 76
    secular work of the
        1670s 51–6, 60–3
    St Paul's cathedral 16, 26–7,
        33, 39–50, 55, 76–8, 82
    surveyor-general of royal
        works, Wren as 20–1,
        26–30, 76
    travels 21–2, 58
    Wadham College, Oxford,
        attendance at 6–7, 19
Wren, Christopher (son) 3, 10,
        14, 20, 45, 47, 67, 75–8,
        82

90

Wren DD, Christopher (father) 1, 2–4, 19

Wren, Faith (née Coghill) (wife) 28, 56–7

Wren, Gilbert (son) 56

'Wren house', concept of 74

Wren, Jane (daughter) 57, 58

Wren, Mary (mother) 1

Wren Society 83–4

Wren, William (son) 57, 58

Enjoy biography? Explore more than 55,000 life stories in the Oxford Dictionary of National Biography

The biographies in the 'Very Interesting People' series derive from the *Oxford Dictionary of National Biography*—available in 60 print volumes and online.

To find out about the lives of more than 55,000 people who shaped all aspects of Britain's past worldwide, visit the *Oxford DNB* website at **www.oxforddnb.com**.

There's lots to discover ...

Read about remarkable people in all walks of life—not just the great and good, but those who left a mark, be they good, bad, or bizarre.

Browse through more than 10,000 portrait illustrations— the largest selection of national portraiture ever published.

Regular features on history in the news—with links to biographies—provide fascinating insights into topical events.

Get a life ... by email

Why not sign up to receive the free *Oxford DNB* 'Life of the Day' by email? Entertaining, informative, and topical biographies delivered direct to your inbox—a great way to start the day.

Find out more at www.oxforddnb.com

'An intellectual wonderland for all scholars and enthusiasts'

Tristram Hunt, *The Times*

The finest scholarship on the greatest people...

Many leading biographers and scholars have contributed
articles on the most influential figures in British history:
for example, Paul Addison on Winston Churchill, Patrick
Collinson on Elizabeth I, Lyndall Gordon on Virginia Woolf,
Christopher Ricks on Alfred Tennyson, Frank Barlow on
Thomas Becket, Fiona MacCarthy on William Morris, Roy
Jenkins on Harold Wilson.

'*Paul Addison's* Churchill ... *is a miniature
masterpiece.*'

Piers Brendon, *The Independent*

Every story fascinates...

The *Oxford DNB* contains stories of courage, malice, romance,
dedication, ambition, and comedy, capturing the diversity
and delights of human conduct. Discover the Irish bishop
who was also an accomplished boomerang thrower, the
historian who insisted on having 'Not Yours' inscribed on
the inside of his hats, and the story of the philanthropist
and friend of Dickens Angela Burdett-Coutts, who defied
convention by proposing to the Duke of Wellington when
he was seventy-seven and she was just thirty. He turned her
down.

'*Every story fascinates. The new ODNB will enrich
your life, and the national life.*'

Matthew Parris, *The Spectator*

www.oxforddnb.com

At 60,000 pages in 60 volumes, the *Oxford Dictionary of National Biography* is one of the largest single works ever printed in English.

The award-winning online edition of the *Oxford DNB* makes it easy to explore the dictionary with great speed and ease. It also provides regular updates of new lives and topical features.

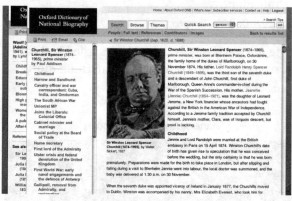

www.oxforddnb.com

The *Oxford Dictionary of National Biography* was created in partnership with the British Academy by scholars of international standing.

It was edited by the late Professor H. C. G. Matthew, Professor of Modern History, University of Oxford, and Professor Sir Brian Harrison, Professor of Modern History, University of Oxford, with the assistance of 14 consultant editors and 470 associate editors worldwide.

Dr Lawrence Goldman, Fellow and Tutor in Modern History, St Peter's College, Oxford, became editor in October 2004.

What readers say

'The *Oxford DNB* is a major work of reference, but it also contains some of the best gossip in the world.'

John Gross, *Sunday Telegraph*

'A fine genealogical research tool that allows you to explore family history, heredity, and even ethnic identity.'

Margaret Drabble, *Prospect*

'The huge website is superbly designed and easy to navigate. Who could ask for anything more?'

Humphrey Carpenter, *Sunday Times*

www.oxforddnb.com